Greetings California!

·H.S.P.·
CALIFORNIA
EXCURSIONS

It gets you there!

HSP CALIFORNIA EXCURSIONS

Your Best Game

Senior Authors

Isabel L. Beck • Roger C. Farr • Dorothy S. Strickland

Authors

Alma Flor Ada • Roxanne F. Hudson • Margaret G. McKeown
Robin C. Scarcella • Julie A. Washington

Harcourt

SCHOOL PUBLISHERS

www.harcourtschool.com

HSP CALIFORNIA EXCURSIONS

Your Best Game

Harcourt
SCHOOL PUBLISHERS

www.harcourtschool.com

Contents

Decodable Story

6

Lesson 18

Social Studies

Social Studies

Theme Big Books

WE'RE GOING ON A **LION HUNT**
David Axtell

Fireflies, Fireflies, Light My Way
By Jonathan London
Illustrated by Linda Messier

READERS' THEATER
Practice Book
Grade 1

"Help Yourself"

Decodable Books 13–18

Comprehension Strategies

Before You Read

Look at the pictures. Think about what you already know.

Set a purpose.

I want to find out about frogs.

While You Read

Ask questions.

What do frogs eat?

Reread.

I'll read this page again.

Answer questions.

Oh! Some frogs eat bugs.

After You Read

Summarize.

First, tadpoles hatch from eggs. Then, they begin changing into frogs. Last, they are full-grown frogs.

Make connections.

This is like another book I read. I learned about how butterflies change.

Theme **4** Wild and Wonderful

Boy Playing with Toys, Steve Dininno

13

Contents

Lesson 13

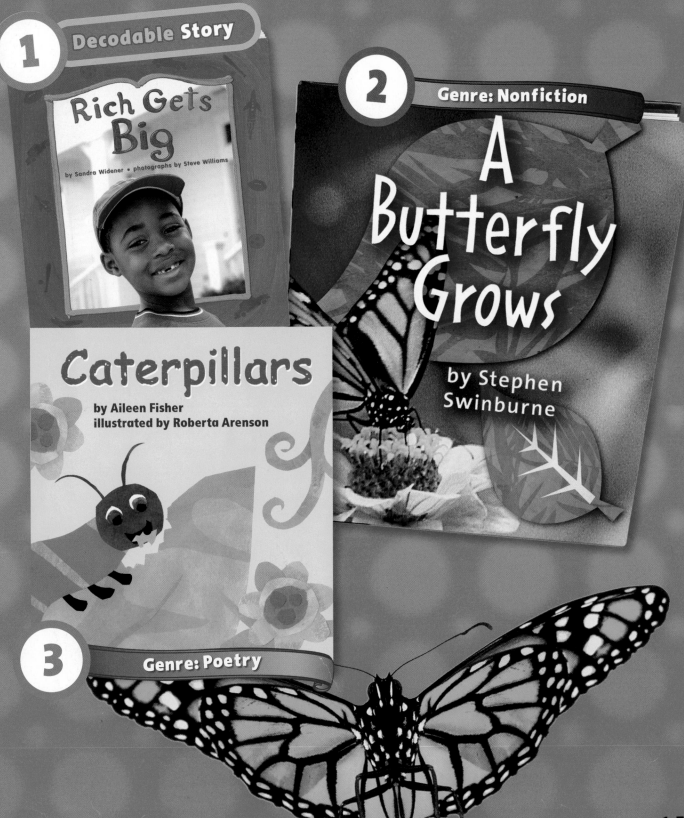

1 Decodable Story

Rich Gets Big
by Sandra Widener • photographs by Steve Williams

2 Genre: Nonfiction

A Butterfly Grows
by Stephen Swinburne

Caterpillars
by Aileen Fisher
illustrated by Roberta Arenson

3 Genre: Poetry

15

Phonics

Words with <u>ch</u> and <u>tch</u>

Words to Know

Review
be
grow
was

Rich Gets Big

by Sandra Widener
photographs by Steve Williams

Rich has a wish to be big.

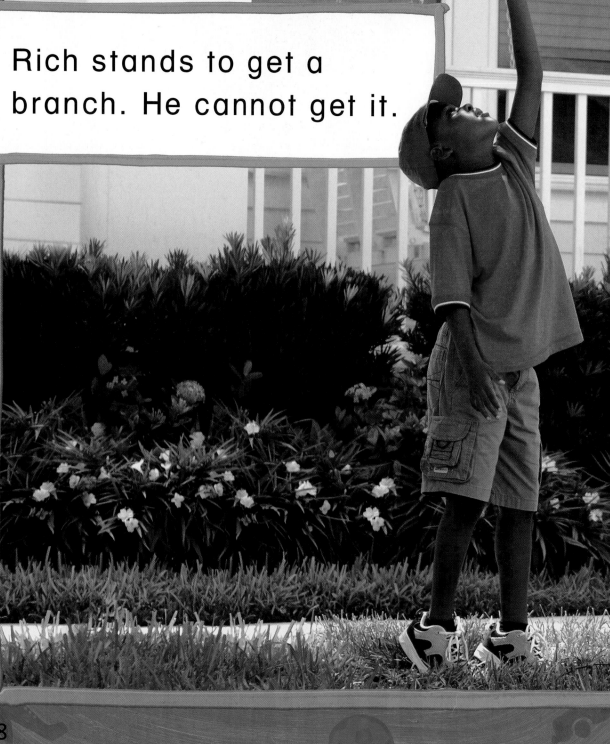

Rich stands to get a branch. He cannot get it.

"Grow just an inch more!" Mom calls.

Rich wants to pitch and catch.
He cannot see the mitt on his
shelf. Mom tells Rich, "You
will not be small for long."

Rich sits on his porch with his cat Patch. He thinks he will not grow.

Mom brings Rich a chest
with snapshots. Mom was
small. Now she is big.

"I will grow!" thinks Rich.
Will Rich get that branch? Yes!
Will Rich get that mitt? Yes!

Focus Skill

 Sequence R2.1

Many nonfiction selections tell about things in the order in which they happen—first, next, and last. This order is called the **sequence**.

Look at the pictures.

They show a sequence of first, next, and last.

 CALIFORNIA STANDARDS
ENGLISH-LANGUAGE ARTS STANDARDS—Reading 2.1 Identify text that uses sequence or other logical order.

Look at the pictures. Do the pictures show a sequence? What happens first, next, and last?

 Try This!

Look at these pictures. Put the pictures in order. Tell what happens first, next, and last.

www.harcourtschool.com/reading

grew

fly

air

friends

play

need

watch

rain

CALIFORNIA STANDARDS
ENGLISH-LANGUAGE ARTS STANDARDS—Reading 1.11 Read
common, irregular sight words (e.g., *the, have, said, come, give, of*).

I **grew** from a small egg. Now I **fly** in the **air** with all my **friends**. Wings help us fly and **play**.

We **need** to drink water. We **watch** for **rain**. Then we sip drops on the plants.

 www.harcourtschool.com/reading

A Butterfly Grows
by Stephen Swinburne

Nonfiction

 Genre Study

Nonfiction selections tell about things that are true. They tell the order in which things happen.

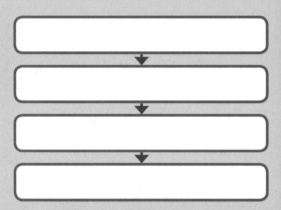

Comprehension Strategy

Use Graphic Organizers

As you read, use a graphic organizer like this to help you understand and remember information in the correct order.

A Butterfly Grows

by Stephen Swinburne

Can you see me
on the plant?

I am a little caterpillar!
I grew in an egg.
Then I hatched!

Wind fills the air. I hang
onto a branch so I don't fall.

32

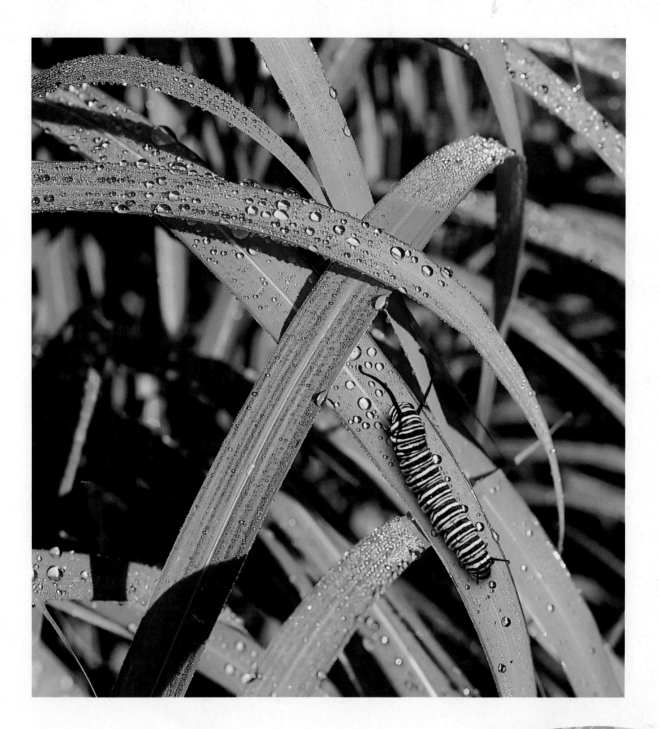

Rain falls. It plips and plops.
I need to drink water.
I drink the small drops.

This plant is my food. I need food so I can grow.

I eat this plant for lunch.
Chomp, chomp!
Crunch, munch!

I eat and grow,
eat and grow.
Now I am big!
My skin is snug.

I look for a spot to rest.
Soon I will shed my skin.

At last I am a chrysalis.
I'm an inch long.
Then in ten days, out I come!

Look at me now!
I am an insect.
I have six legs.

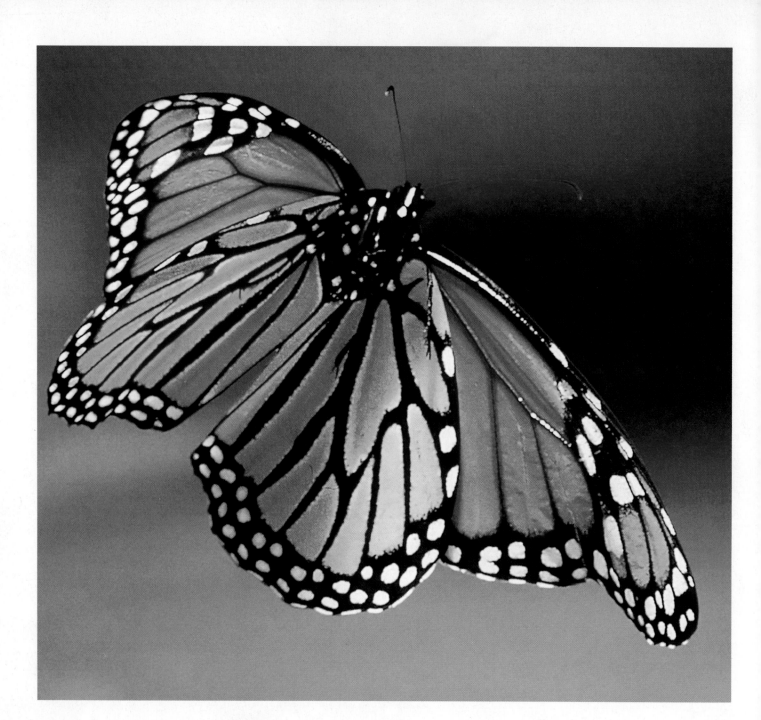

My wings help me fly.
Watch me fly!

I like to fly with all my friends.
Wings help us play.
Wings help us to go find plants for food.

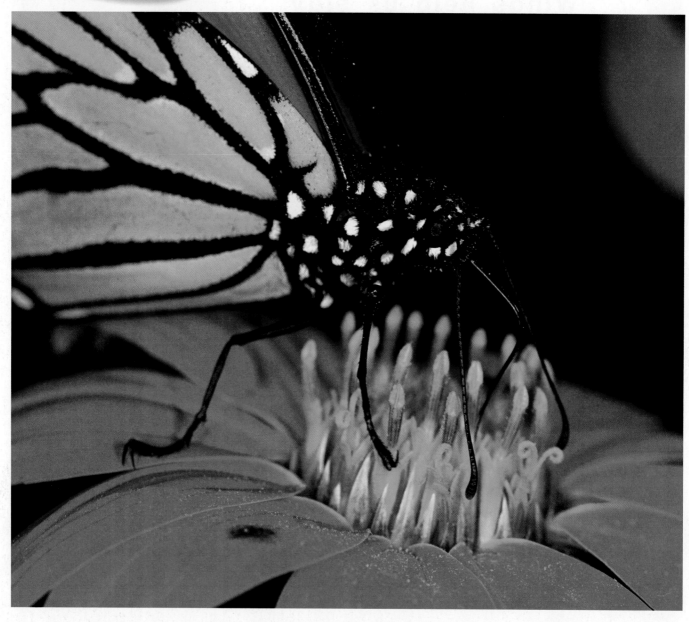

Watch me eat now!
I sip and sip.

I am a butterfly!
I'm a beautiful butterfly!

Think Critically

R2.1
R2.6
R2.7
R3.2
W2.1

1 How does the caterpillar change in this story? SEQUENCE

2 Why does the caterpillar eat so much? DETAILS

3 Why does the caterpillar come out of its chrysalis? DRAW CONCLUSIONS

4 Why do you think the author has the butterfly tell its own story?

AUTHOR'S PURPOSE

5 **WRITE** Imagine that you are a caterpillar or a butterfly for a day. Write about what you do.

 WRITING RESPONSE

Meet the Author/Photographer
Stephen Swinburne

Stephen Swinburne loves nature—
especially butterflies! He planted a
garden at his house filled with flowers
that butterflies like. He took many of
the pictures for "A Butterfly Grows"
in his garden. He hopes you enjoy
learning about butterflies!

 www.harcourtschool.com/reading

45

Poetry

Caterpillars

by Aileen Fisher
illustrated by Roberta Arenson

What do caterpillars do?
Nothing much but chew and chew.

What do caterpillars know?
Nothing much but how to grow.

They just eat what by and by
will make them be a butterfly,

But that is more than I can do
however much I chew and chew.

47

Connections

Comparing Texts

R2.2
R2.7
LS1.5

1 What do the story and the poem say a caterpillar must do to grow?

2 Tell about a butterfly or another bug you have seen. What did it do?

3 How have you changed as you have grown?

Writing

W2.2

Think about the story. Write three sentences to tell how a butterfly grows.

First, the egg _____.
Next, the caterpillar _____.
Last, the caterpillar _____.

CALIFORNIA STANDARDS
ENGLISH-LANGUAGE ARTS STANDARDS—Reading 1.10 Generate the sounds from all the letters and letter patterns, including consonant blends and long- and short-vowel patterns (i.e., phonograms), and blend those sounds into recognizable words; **Reading 1.16** Read aloud with fluency in a manner that sounds like natural speech; *(continued)*

Make and read new words.

Start with **chin**.

Switch | c | h | and | i | n |.

Add | p | in front of | i |.

Change | n | to | t |.

Change | i | to | a |.

Read the story aloud with a partner. Make your voice go up or down. Make it loud or soft to sound as if the butterfly is really talking.

I am a butterfly!

I'm a beautiful butterfly!

Reading 2.2 Respond to *who, what, when, where,* and *how* questions; **Reading 2.7** Retell the central ideas of simple expository or narrative passages; **Writing 2.2** Write brief expository descriptions of a real object, person, place, or event, using sensory details; **Listening and Speaking 1.5** Use descriptive words when speaking about people, places, things, and events.

Reading-Writing Connection

Responding to a Selection

"A Butterfly Grows" is a nonfiction selection about how butterflies grow and change. We read the selection. Then we wrote about what we knew and what we learned.

▶ **First, we talked about the selection.**

▶ **Next, we named things we already knew and things we learned.**

▶ **Last, we read our sentences.**

What We Knew
Caterpillars change into butterflies.

Butterflies have six legs.

What We Learned
Caterpillars eat leaves and drink drops of water.

A butterfly is in a chrysalis for ten days.

Contents

Lesson 14

1 Decodable Story

Ann's Trip to the Stars
by Karen Sandoval   illustrated by Olivier Latyk

2 Genre: Realistic Fiction

Mark's Big Day
by Monica Greenfield
illustrated by Shane Evans

Putting on a Play

3 Genre: Nonfiction

Phonics
Words with <u>ar</u>

Words to Know

Review

play

says

her

cold

Ann's Trip to the Stars

by Karen Sandoval

illustrated by Olivier Latyk

"Dad, will you help with my play?" asks Ann.

"Yes!" says Dad.

Dad hangs cloth in the hall.

"I am off to the stars!" grins Ann.
"My ship will go far in a flash."

Ann starts her long trip.
"The sun is big and hot," says Ann.
"Mars is red. It can get cold."

"My ship crashes!" Ann yells. "It is dark. Sharp rocks block my path."

"My ship will not start," says Ann.

Bark! Bark!

"Carl has a kit to fix it!"

"I fix my ship and blast off! I am back," says Ann. "The end!"

Dad claps. Mom claps. Ben stands
and claps, and Carl barks.
"Thanks!" says Ann with a big grin.

Phonics Skill

Words with ar

The letters **ar** can stand for the sound at the beginning of the words **art** and **arm**.

art   arm

The letters **ar** can stand for the same sound in the middle of **yarn** and at the end of **star**.

yarn   star

CALIFORNIA STANDARDS
ENGLISH-LANGUAGE ARTS STANDARDS—Reading 1.10 Generate the sounds from all the letters and letter patterns, including consonant blends and long- and short-vowel patterns (i.e., phonograms), and blend those sounds into recognizable words; **Reading 1.12** Use knowledge of vowel digraphs and r-controlled letter-sound associations to read words.

Look at each picture. Read the words.
Tell which word names the picture.

card

cart

cord

scar

sort

scarf

GO online www.harcourtschool.com/reading

Try This!

Read the story.

We went to a farm in the car. It was very far. We saw animals at the barn. We went on a cart. At night, we saw some stars.

63

Words to Know

R1.11

feel

put

house

Mrs.

say

loud

again

know

CALIFORNIA STANDARDS
ENGLISH-LANGUAGE ARTS STANDARDS—Reading 1.11 Read common, irregular sight words (e.g., *the, have, said, come, give, of*).

"I **feel** a chill in the air," said Mark. He **put** on a hat. He left the **house** and went to school.

At school, **Mrs.** Parks said, "**Say** your part, Mark. Be **loud**." Mark said his part.

"Now say it **again**. I **know** you can do a good job!" she said.

 www.harcourtschool.com/reading

Mark's Big Day
by Monica Greenfield
illustrated by Shane Evans

Realistic Fiction

R3.1

Genre Study
Realistic fiction stories are made-up, but have characters like people we know.

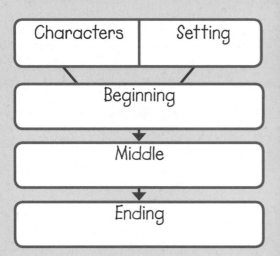

Characters	Setting

Beginning

Middle

Ending

R2.7

Comprehension Strategy
Summarize As you read, stop every few pages and think about the important things that have happened so far.

CALIFORNIA STANDARDS
ENGLISH-LANGUAGE ARTS STANDARDS—Reading
2.7 Retell the central ideas of simple expository or narrative passages; **Reading 3.1** Identify and describe the elements of plot, setting, and character(s) in a story, as well as the story's beginning, middle, and ending.

Mark's Big Day

by Monica Greenfield

illustrated
by Shane Evans

Mark's clock went <u>bing</u>, <u>bing</u>, <u>bing</u>.
He did not want to get up.

Bing! Bing! Bing!

68

Mom called, "Mark, get up and
get dressed. It's your big day!"

Mark was thinking of the school play.
His part was hard for him. He felt shy.
Mark put on his jacket, hat, and scarf.

"Wish me luck," Mark said. He got a big
hug from Mom. His dog barked.
"Thanks, Mom. Thanks, Champ," Mark said
with a grin.

At school, Mrs. Parks asked
the children to say their parts.

73

"I'll huff and I'll puff and I'll blow your house in," Mark said. It was too soft.

"Say it again, Mark," Mrs. Parks called.
"I'll blow your house in," Mark said.
It was soft again.

"You are the wolf. This wolf is not shy," said Mrs. Parks.

"This is hard, but I know you can do it, Mark. Just act like a big wolf."

The play started. Soon it was time for Mark to say his part.

"I'll huff and I'll puff and I'll blow your house OUT!" he called.

The children looked at Mark.
He had made a mistake.

"Oh! I'll huff and I'll puff and
I'll blow your house IN!" Mark said
with a big wolf snarl.

81

"Don't feel bad, Mark,"
Mrs. Parks said.

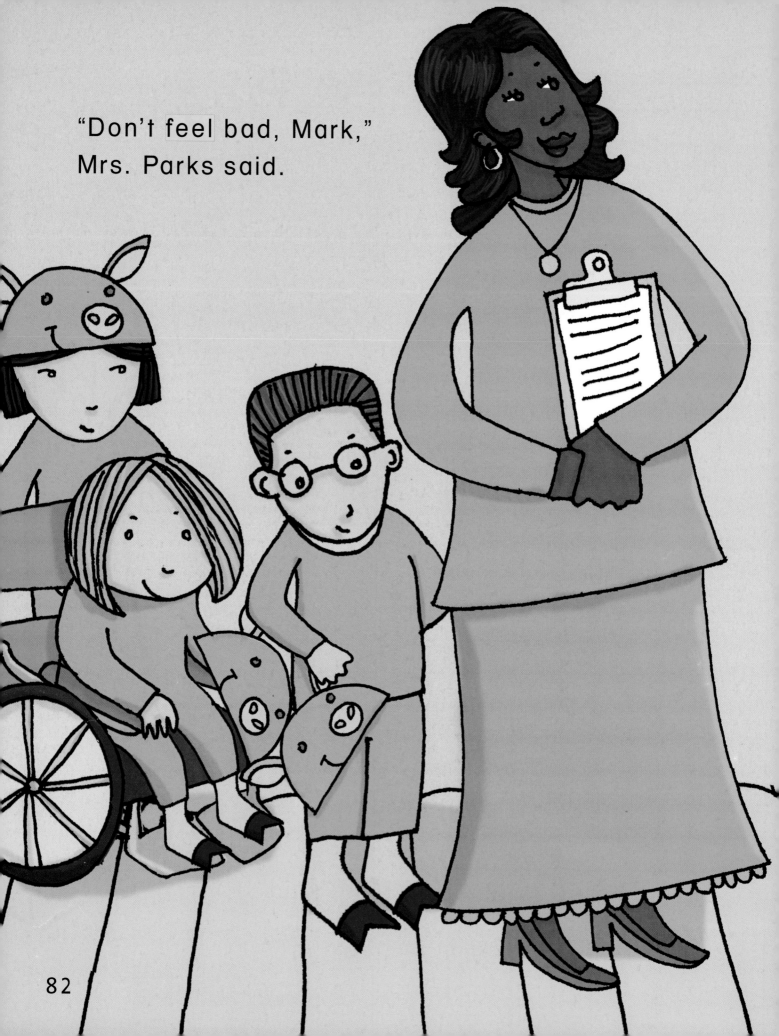

"I don't," Mark said. "I feel good."
"You do?" asked Mrs. Parks.

"Yes! I wasn't shy. I was LOUD!"
Mark said with a big grin.

Think Critically

R2.2
R2.7
R3.1
R3.2
W2.2

1 What do you think the author wanted you to learn from the story?

AUTHOR'S PURPOSE/POINT OF VIEW

2 Who helps Mark at home? Who helps Mark at school? DETAILS

3 Why do you think Mark says his part softly at first? MAKE INFERENCES

4 Why is Mark able to say his part loudly during the play? DRAW CONCLUSIONS

5 **WRITE** Write about how you would act as the wolf in a play. What kind of costume would you wear? WRITING RESPONSE

CALIFORNIA STANDARDS
ENGLISH-LANGUAGE ARTS STANDARDS—Reading 2.2 Respond to *who, what, when, where,* and *how* questions; **Reading 2.7** Retell the central ideas of simple expository or narrative passages; **Reading 3.1** Identify and describe the elements of plot, setting, and character(s) in a story, as well as the story's beginning, middle, and ending; **Reading 3.2** Describe the roles of authors and illustrators and their contributions to print materials; **Writing 2.2** Write brief expository descriptions of a real object, person, place, or event, using sensory details.

85

Meet the Author
Monica Greenfield

Monica Greenfield comes from a family of writers. Her mother writes stories and poems, and so did her grandmother. Her daughter loves to write, also.

"Words can be very powerful. I can use words to make children laugh, give them something to think about, or let them know how strong they are."

Meet the Illustrator

Shane Evans

Shane Evans has illustrated many children's books. He has created art for people all over the world. His art has been shown in Africa, Paris, New York, and Chicago. Mr. Evans also likes to speak at schools. He encourages children to use their own special talents.

87

Putting on a Play

Many people work together to put on a play.

The **Director** is in charge. He or she tells everyone what to do.

88

The **Set Designer** is in charge of how the stage will look for the play.

Actors and Actresses need to know how to pretend. They use words and actions to tell a story.

The **Costume Designer** makes the clothes that the actors and actresses wear.

Which job would you like to have? Why?

89

Connections

Comparing Texts

1 What job from "Putting on a Play" do you think Mark would like? Why?

2 Tell what you liked about Mark's play or about a play you have seen.

3 What would you tell a friend who felt shy or afraid?

Writing

Mark felt proud of himself. Write about something you have done that you are proud of.

I am proud of how I take care of my baby brother.

CALIFORNIA STANDARDS
ENGLISH-LANGUAGE ARTS STANDARDS—Reading 1.10 Generate the sounds from all the letters and letter patterns, including consonant blends and long- and short-vowel patterns (i.e., phonograms), and blend those sounds into recognizable words; **Reading 1.12** Use knowledge of vowel digraphs and r-controlled letter-sound associations to read words; *(continued)*

Phonics

Make and read new words.

Start with **far**.

Add **m** to the end.

Take away the **f**.

Change **m** to **t**.

Add **p** to the beginning.

Fluency Practice

Read the story aloud with a partner. Read softly where Mark speaks softly. Read like the Big Bad Wolf where Mark does!

I'll huff and I'll puff . . .

Reading 1.16 Read aloud with fluency in a manner that sounds like natural speech; **Reading 2.2** Respond to *who, what, when, where,* and *how* questions; **Reading 2.6** Relate prior knowledge to textual information; **Writing 2.1** Write brief narratives (e.g., fictional, autobiographical) describing an experience; **Listening and Speaking 1.5** Use descriptive words when speaking about people, places, things, and events.

91

Contents

Lesson 15

1 Decodable Story

A Quiz for Brent

by Karen Sandoval • Illustrated by Joe Cepeda

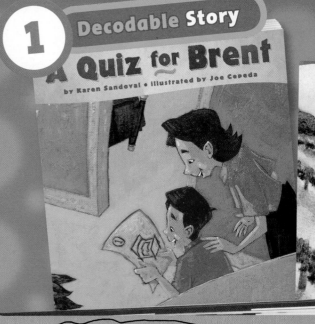

2 Genre: Biography

Tomás Rivera

by Jane Medina

illustrated by
René King Moreno

3 Genre: Poetry

I Can

by Mari Evans

illustrated by
Shane Evans

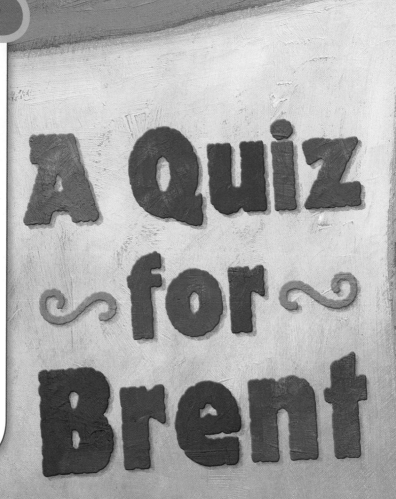

A Quiz for Brent

by Karen Sandoval

illustrated by
Joe Cepeda

Mom has a quiz for Brent. Brent gets a hint. "Check the bed, Brent," Mom tells him.

Think, Brent, think!
A small, red bucket is
on the soft quilt. Brent
is glad he got that hint.

Dad has a quiz for Brent.
Brent gets a hint.

"Check the desk, Brent,"
Dad tells him.

Think, Brent, think!
A big, tan cloth is on the
desk. Brent is happy he got
that hint, too.

What will Brent **find**? Is it Mom?
Is it Dad? Brent will finish his
quiz out of the **house**.

Brent will not quit.
He runs to the yard!
Quick, Brent, quick!

It's Granddad! Brent is glad he did not quit!

Focus Skill

Sequence

Authors tell about things in the order in which they happen. The order makes sense. This order is called the **sequence**.

Look at the pictures.

They show a sequence of first, next, and last.

 CALIFORNIA STANDARDS
ENGLISH-LANGUAGE ARTS STANDARDS—Reading 2.1 Identify text that uses sequence or other logical order.

Look at the pictures. Do they show a sequence? What happens first, next, and last?

 Try This!

Look at these pictures. Put them in order.
Tell what happens first, next, and last.

GO online www.harcourtschool.com/reading

Words to Know

R1.11

books

about

read

work

writing

people

family

name

 CALIFORNIA STANDARDS
ENGLISH-LANGUAGE ARTS STANDARDS—Reading 1.11 Read common, irregular sight words (e.g., *the, have, said, come, give, of*).

I have **books about** cars and trucks. It is fun to **read** lots of books.

I like to **work** on stories, too. I am **writing** one to tell **people** about my **family**. It is hard work, but I like it! I will put my **name** on it.

GO online www.harcourtschool.com/reading

Tomás Rivera

by Jane Medina
Illustrated by
René King Moreno

Biography

Genre Study

A **biography** is a story about the events in the life of a real person.

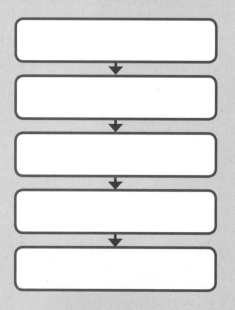

Comprehension Strategy

Ask Questions As you read, ask yourself questions and look for the answers.

106

Tomás Rivera

by Jane Medina

illustrated by
René King Moreno

Tomás Rivera was born in Texas.
Tomás and his family went from
farm to farm picking crops.

Tomás helped pick crops all day.
It was hard work. At night he had
fun with his Grandpa.

"Come quick, children!" Grandpa called.
"It's time for stories!"

"You tell the best stories!"
Tomás said. "I want to tell
good stories, too."

"We can get lots of stories
for you, Tomás," said Grandpa.
"When?" asked Tomás.

"Let's go now!" Grandpa said
with a wink. "Quick, hop in!"

"This is a library," said Grandpa.
"Look at all the books!" gasped
Tomás as he clapped his hands.

"Read all you can, Tomás. It will help you think of lots of stories," said Grandpa.

Tomás read lots and lots of books.
He read about bugs, stars, and cars.
Tomás started thinking of stories.

Tomás started telling his stories.
Then he started writing them.

When he grew up, Tomás got a job as a teacher. He still kept writing stories.

Tomás Rivera's stories tell about people picking crops, just as his family did. Lots of people read his books.

Now his name is on a big library.
Many people visit the library.
They get books, just as Tomás did.

Think Critically

R2.1
R2.6
R2.7
W2.1

1. How does Tomás feel about books after he goes to the library with Grandpa? SEQUENCE

2. Why does Grandpa want Tomás to read lots of books? MAKE INFERENCES

3. How does Tomás learn to tell stories? PLOT

4. Why do you think Tomás Rivera wrote stories about people picking crops? DRAW CONCLUSIONS

5. **WRITE** Write about a job you would like to have someday. WRITING RESPONSE

CALIFORNIA STANDARDS
ENGLISH-LANGUAGE ARTS STANDARDS—Reading 2.1 Identify text that uses sequence or other logical order; **Reading 2.6** Relate prior knowledge to textual information; **Reading 2.7** Retell the central ideas of simple expository or narrative passages; **Writing 2.1** Write brief narratives (e.g., fictional, autobiographical) describing an experience.

Meet the Author
Jane Medina

Jane Medina read a lot about Tomás Rivera so that she could tell this story about his life. She hopes the story will help children think as Tomás Rivera did.

"If you work hard and do well in school, you can do anything you want to do!"

Meet the Illustrator
René King Moreno

When René King Moreno was young, she loved to spend her spare time drawing and painting. She studied art in school, and now she illustrates children's books.

 www.harcourtschool.com/reading

I Can
by Mari Evans
illustrated by
Shane Evans

Poetry

by Mari Evans
illustrated by
Shane Evans

I Can

I can
be anything
I can
do anything
I can
think
anything
big
or tall
OR
high or low
W I D E
or narrow
fast or slow
because I
CAN
and
I
WANT
TO!

125

Connections

Comparing Texts
R2.2
R2.7
R3.3

❶ How is Tomás like the girl in the poem "I Can"?

❷ Why is it important to believe you can do the things you want to do?

❸ What things did Tomás do that you also like to do?

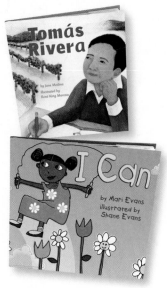

Writing
W2.1

Write about something special you did with a family member or friend. Tell what happened first, next, and last.

One day, my dad and I went to the park. We played basketball together. I won! Then we ate ice cream cones. It was fun!

CALIFORNIA STANDARDS
ENGLISH-LANGUAGE ARTS STANDARDS—Reading 1.10 Generate the sounds from all the letters and letter patterns, including consonant blends and long- and short-vowel patterns (i.e., phonograms), and blend those sounds into recognizable words; Reading 1.16 Read aloud with fluency in a manner that sounds like natural speech; (continued)

Make and read new words.

Start with **quick**.

Change i to a .

Change q u to w h .

Change c k to t .

Change a t to e n .

Read "Tomás Rivera" with a classmate. Take turns reading the pages. Read the easy parts quickly. Read the harder parts more slowly.

Reading 2.2 Respond to *who, what, when, where,* and *how* questions; **Reading 2.7** Retell the central ideas of simple expository or narrative passages; **Reading 3.3** Recollect, talk, and write about books read during the school year; **Writing 2.1** Write brief narratives (e.g., fictional, autobiographical) describing an experience.

Contents

Lesson 16

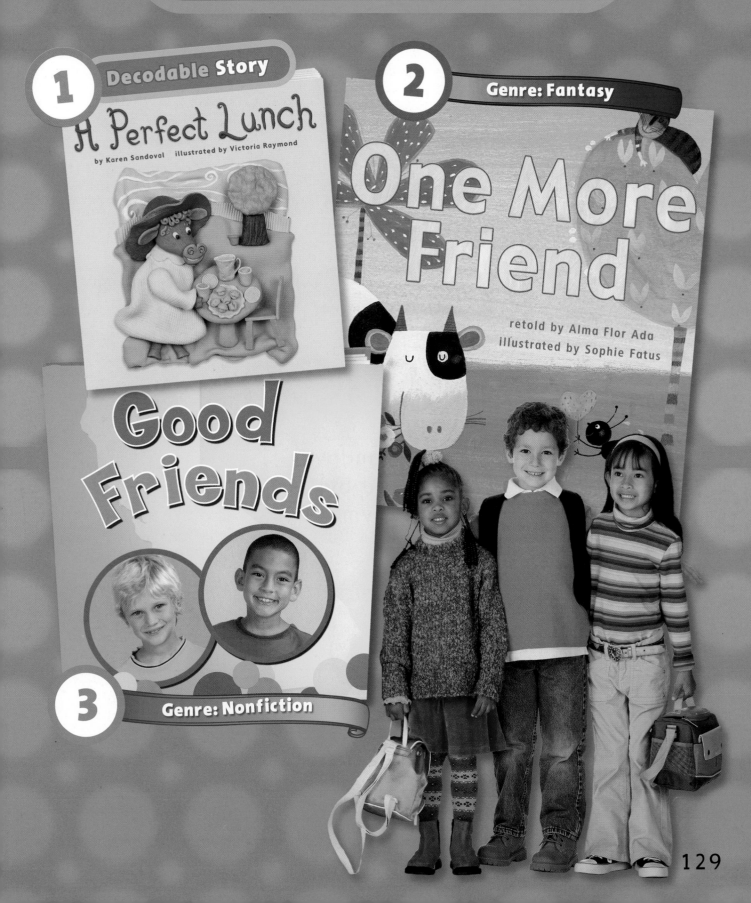

1 Decodable Story

A Perfect Lunch

by Karen Sandoval   illustrated by Victoria Raymond

Good Friends

3 Genre: Nonfiction

2 Genre: Fantasy

One More Friend

retold by Alma Flor Ada
illustrated by Sophie Fatus

Phonics
Words with <u>er</u> and <u>ir</u>

Words to Know

Review

says

oh

no

now

friends

A Perfect Lunch

by Karen Sandoval
illustrated by
Victoria Raymond

"Come for lunch," says Meg.
She is serving corn muffins.
Meg sets out her best dishes.
"How charming!" she grins.

Ben comes first. He sits
with Meg. Ben fills his glass.
Squirt! He squirts Meg.
"Oh, no!" yells Ben.

Liz is next. She sits with Ben.
Liz picks up her muffin, and her
skirt bumps Ben.

Kit is third. She sits with Liz. Kit sips
her drink and drops her muffin in the
dirt. Meg's big hat brim hits Ben.

Here is Jen. Where can this bird sit? Perhaps this twig will do the trick. Liz looks up and bumps Meg's hat.

Tap, tap, tap! It's Bert!

"Oh, no! Where will Bert sit?"
they all ask.

"Let's have a picnic!" says Bert.

"It's a perfect day now with all my friends," Meg says. Meg and all her friends have a perfect lunch!

Main Idea

What a story is mostly about is the **main idea**.

Look at the picture.

The main idea is that a family is having dinner.

CALIFORNIA STANDARDS
ENGLISH-LANGUAGE ARTS STANDARDS—Reading 2.7 Retell the central ideas of simple expository or narrative passages.

Look at the picture. What is the main idea? How do you know?

Try This!

Look at this picture. Tell what you think the main idea is.

www.harcourtschool.com/reading

Words to Know

High-Frequency Words

Cow's

nice

by

please

join

always

room

 CALIFORNIA STANDARDS
ENGLISH-LANGUAGE ARTS STANDARDS—Reading 1.11 Read common, irregular sight words (e.g., *the, have, said, come, give, of*).

Ant, Frog, and Chick like to be in **Cow's** yard. They think it's **nice** to sit **by** their friends. Here comes Hen.

"**Please** come and **join** us!" the animals say. They **always** make **room** for one more friend.

GO online www.harcourtschool.com/reading

One More Friend

retold by Alma Flor Ada
illustrated by Sophie Fatus

Fantasy

R3.1

Genre Study

A **fantasy** is a story that has make-believe characters and events.

R2.7

Comprehension Strategy

Summarize As you read, stop every few pages and think about the important things that have happened so far.

CALIFORNIA STANDARDS
ENGLISH-LANGUAGE ARTS STANDARDS—Reading
2.7 Retell the central ideas of simple expository or narrative passages; **Reading 3.1** Identify and describe the elements of plot, setting, and character(s) in a story, as well as the story's beginning, middle, and ending.

142

One More Friend

retold by Alma Flor Ada

illustrated by Sophie Fatus

"My, it's nice to rest in the shade!"
Ant is happy in the hammock in Cow's
backyard.

Frog hops up. "Ribbit ribbit!"
"Jump up, Frog! Be the first!" calls Ant.
"There's always room for one more.
Please don't say you can't!"

Chick skips by. "Chirp chirp!"
"Come join us, little bird!" calls Ant.
"There's always room for one more.
Please don't say you can't!"

Hen steps up. "Cluck cluck!"
"Come join us! Be the third!" calls Ant.
"There's always room for one more.
Please don't say you can't!"

Duck flaps his wings. "Quack quack!"
"Come join us, good sir!" calls Ant.
"There's always room for one more.
Please don't say you can't!"

"My, it's nice to rest in the shade!"
Ant, Frog, Chick, Hen, and Duck are
all happy in the hammock in Cow's
backyard.

Cat slinks by in the grass. "Purr purr!"
"Come join us and curl up!" calls Ant.
"There's always room for one more.
Please don't say you can't!"

Dog and Lamb run up. "Bark bark! Baaa baaa!"
"Come join us! It's your turn!" calls Ant.
"There's always room for one more.
Please don't say you can't!"

"My, it's nice to rest in the shade!"
Ant, Frog, Chick, Hen, Duck, Cat, Dog,
and Lamb are all happy in the hammock
in Cow's backyard.

Then up jumps Cow.
Who is this now?
It's a big elephant!
What will Ant say?
Oh, no! She can't. . .

But Ant calls out,
"Come join us!"

When there is kindness,
there's always a way
for one more friend
to join in and play!

Think Critically

R2.6
R2.7
R3.1
W2.1

1 How does Ant show kindness?

MAIN IDEA

2 What other animal in the story is kind? Why do you think so? DRAW CONCLUSIONS

3 Who does Ant invite into the hammock? DETAILS

4 What are the animals worried about when the elephant comes by? MAKE INFERENCES

5 **WRITE** Write about one way you can be kind to others. WRITING RESPONSE

CALIFORNIA STANDARDS
ENGLISH-LANGUAGE ARTS STANDARDS—Reading 2.6 Relate prior knowledge to textual information; **Reading 2.7** Retell the central ideas of simple expository or narrative passages; **Reading 3.1** Identify and describe the elements of plot, setting, and character(s) in a story, as well as the story's beginning, middle, and ending; **Writing 2.1** Write brief narratives (e.g., fictional, autobiographical) describing an experience.

Meet the Author
Alma Flor Ada

The ideas for "One More Friend" come from Alma Flor Ada's childhood. She loved hammocks as a child in Cuba, and slept on them many times. Also, at her house they were always making room at the table for a relative or visitor. Her cousin would often say, "There's always room for one more!"

Meet the Illustrator
Sophie Fatus

Sophie Fatus is an artist who grew up in France and now lives in Italy. She loves animals and enjoys painting them very much, like the ones in this story. She hopes that her artwork will help children remember to like each other and be kind to one another.

GO online www.harcourtschool.com/reading

Good Friends

Nonfiction

Good Friends

Justin lives in Sacramento, California.
Reed lives in Patterson, California.

Sacramento

Patterson

They are good friends even
though they live far apart.

160

Justin likes living in Sacramento because it has tall buildings and busy streets.

Reed likes living around all the farms and wide open spaces in Patterson.

Best of all, Justin and Reed like spending time together.

Connections

Comparing Texts

R2.2
R3.1
R3.3

1 Did you like "One More Friend" or "Good Friends" better? Why?

2 Think of a person you know who is like Ant. How is this person like Ant?

3 How would you be kind to someone?

Writing

Write a note to invite a friend to your house. List the things you plan to do when he or she visits.

Main Idea
things to do for
fun with my friend

Details

ride bikes

eat a snack

play with my dog

CALIFORNIA STANDARDS
ENGLISH-LANGUAGE ARTS STANDARDS—Reading 1.10 Generate the sounds from all the letters and letter patterns, including consonant blends and long- and short-vowel patterns (i.e., phonograms), and blend those sounds into recognizable words; *(continued)*

Make and read new words.

Start with the word **sir**.

Change **s** to **b**. Add **d** to the end.

Change **b** to **t** **h**.

Take off **t**. Change **i** to **e**.

Change **e** to **u** and **d** to **t**.

Fluency Practice R1.16

Read "One More Friend" with a classmate. Read each sentence together. Read at a steady pace. Try to keep the rhythm of the words.

There's always room for one more.

Please don't say you can't!

Reading 1.12 Use knowledge of vowel digraphs and r-controlled letter-sound associations to read words; **Reading 1.16** Read aloud with fluency in a manner that sounds like natural speech; **Reading 2.2** Respond to *who, what, when, where,* and *how* questions; **Reading 3.1** Identify and describe the elements of plot, setting, and character(s) in a story, as well as the story's beginning, middle, and ending; **Reading 3.3** Recollect, talk, and write about books read during the school year.

Contents

Lesson 17

1 Decodable Story

Jungle Fun
by Nancy Furstinger
illustrated by Michelle Angers

2 Genre: Nonfiction

Can Elephants Paint?
by Katya Arnold

3 Genre: Nonfiction Article

An Elephant's Three T's

Phonics
Words with <u>le</u>

Words to Know

Review

soon

animals

make

family

join

Jungle Fun

by Nancy Furstinger

illustrated by
Michelle Angers

A contest will start soon. The contest is in the jungle. The animals will do fun tricks. Who will win?

Big cats run and jump and tumble.
Little cats giggle and chuckle.

Big red foxes juggle balls and pins.
Little red foxes cannot catch the
balls and pins.

Big birds ring bells that jingle jangle. Little birds chirp and make bubbles.

An elephant family will join in the fun. They have purple hats that glitter and sparkle.

Big elephants stomp and kick.
Little elephants wiggle and turn
and spin.

Big animals and little animals all have fun! Who can do the best tricks?

You pick!

Focus Skill

 Main Idea R2.7

The **main idea** of a story is the most important idea.

Look at the picture.

The main idea is that a boy is learning to tie his shoes.

 CALIFORNIA STANDARDS
ENGLISH-LANGUAGE ARTS STANDARDS—Reading 2.7 Retell the central ideas of simple expository or narrative passages.

Look at the picture. What is the main idea? How do you know?

Try This!

Look at the picture. Choose the words that name the main idea.

● working on a farm

● working at school

● working at home

 www.harcourtschool.com/reading

175

Words to Know

High-Frequency Words

R1.11

would

carry

other

money

buy

paint

paper

 CALIFORNIA STANDARDS
ENGLISH-LANGUAGE ARTS STANDARDS—Reading 1.11 Read common, irregular sight words (e.g., *the, have, said, come, give, of*).

The elephants on a farm had jobs. They **would carry** trees with their trunks.

An artist met an elephant named Lucky. The artist liked Lucky and the **other** elephants on the farm.

The artist used **money** to **buy** things for the elephants. Now they have **paint**, brushes, and **paper**.

Can Elephants Paint?
by Katya Arnold

Nonfiction

Genre Study

R2.7

A **nonfiction** selection gives true information about a main idea. It often has photographs.

Main Idea

Details

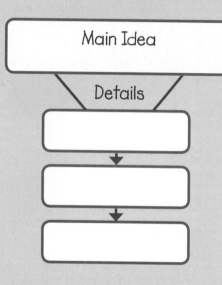

Comprehension Strategy

Monitor Comprehension: Reread If you read a part that you don't understand, go back and read it again.

CALIFORNIA STANDARDS
ENGLISH-LANGUAGE ARTS STANDARDS—
Reading 2.7 Retell the central ideas of simple expository or narrative passages.

Can Elephants Paint?

a true story by Katya Arnold

Lucky lived on a farm.
She was big and strong.

All the elephants on that farm had jobs. They worked in the jungle.

Ning worked with Lucky. Ning cut trees. Then Lucky would carry them off with her trunk.

Ning and Lucky worked hard to get money.

On days off, they would swim.

One day, all the big trees were cut. There were no more jobs. "What will we do?" asked Ning.

An artist had a good idea.
"I think I can help them," she
said. The artist went to the farm.

"I use my hands when I paint. Elephants can use their trunks," said the artist. She dipped a brush in purple.

Lucky grabbed the handle
with her trunk.
"Good!" said the artist. "Let's
paint, Lucky!"

Lucky made a little spot.
The artist started to giggle.
"Not on your head, darling!
Watch me."

The artist dragged the brush on the paper. Then she handed it back to Lucky. Lucky blinked.

"You can do it!" said the artist.

Lucky made a little purple
dot in the middle.
"You are an artist, Lucky!"

Then the artist held Lucky's trunk.
She helped Lucky paint lines, wiggles,
splashes, and little dots.

Other elephants came by. The artist handed them all brushes.

"How can this help us get money?" Ning was thinking.

This elephant painted lots of marks with her brush.

Others liked lines and spots.
They made them thin and thick,
short and long, pink and black.

One painted simple flowers.

A little one just wanted to nibble his brush.

People saw this art and said,
"It's so nice!"
They wanted to buy the art.
They hung it in their homes.

"Thank you for helping us!"
Ning said to the artist.
Now they all had new jobs.

R2.1
R2.2
R2.7
W2.2

Think Critically

1 Why was it a good idea for the elephants to learn to paint?

 MAIN IDEA

2 What is Lucky's home like? DETAILS

3 How does Ning feel when all the big trees are gone? Why? DRAW CONCLUSIONS

4 Think about the beginning and the end of this selection. How does Lucky's life change? MAKE INFERENCES

5 **WRITE** Write about something else an elephant could learn to do.

WRITING RESPONSE

 CALIFORNIA STANDARDS
ENGLISH-LANGUAGE ARTS STANDARDS—Reading 2.1 Identify text that uses sequence or other logical order; **Reading 2.2** Respond to *who, what, when, where,* and *how* questions; **Reading 2.7** Retell the central ideas of simple expository or narrative passages; **Writing 2.2** Write brief expository descriptions of a real object, person, place, or event, using sensory details.

Meet the Author/Photographer
Katya Arnold

Katya Arnold teaches art to children in New York—and to elephants in Asia! Her husband Alex is also an artist. Together, they helped the elephants create amazing paintings.

Some elephants painted for a long time. Others just played with the brushes. But they all liked to sneak snacks out of the artists' pockets with their trunks!

 GO online www.harcourtschool.com/reading

199

Science

An
Elephant's
Three
T's

Nonfiction Article

Teacher Read-Aloud

An Elephant's Three T's

Teeth

Animals that eat plants have flat teeth. Elephants use their flat teeth to chew leaves, twigs, fruit, and bark.

Tusks

Elephant tusks are long teeth. They are made of ivory. Elephants can use their tusks to help get food.

Trunk

Elephants breathe through their trunks. They also use their trunks to put food and water in their mouths. They can even take a shower.

Best of all, elephants use their trunks to give each other a hug!

Connections

Comparing Texts

R2.2
R3.3
LS1.5

1 What is the most interesting thing you learned from the selection and the article?

2 Tell about an elephant that you have seen. What did it do?

3 What is your favorite way to make pictures? Tell how you do it.

Can Elephants Paint?
by Katya Arnold

An Elephant's Three T's

Writing
W2.2

Write notes telling what you know about elephants. Then write sentences.

Elephants can pick up things with their strong trunks.

Main Idea
Things I know about elephants

Details

pick up things with their trunks

have teeth

some paint pictures

CALIFORNIA STANDARDS
ENGLISH-LANGUAGE ARTS STANDARDS—Reading 1.10 Generate the sounds from all the letters and letter patterns, including consonant blends and long- and short-vowel patterns (i.e., phonograms), and blend those sounds into recognizable words; **Reading 1.16** Read aloud with fluency in a manner that sounds like natural speech; *(continued)*

Make and read new words.

Start with **little**.

Change **l** to **w** and **t** **t** to **g** **g**.

Change **w** to **g**.

Change **gigg** to **cand**.

Change **c** to **h**.

Read "Can Elephants Paint?" aloud to a partner. Pause when you see a comma or a period. Use your voice to show excitement when there is an exclamation point.

Let's paint, Lucky!

Reading 2.2 Respond to *who, what, when, where,* and *how* questions; **Reading 3.3** Recollect, talk, and write about books read during the school year; **Writing 2.2** Write brief expository descriptions of a real object, person, place, or event, using sensory details; **Listening and Speaking 1.5** Use descriptive words when speaking about people, places, things, and events.

Contents

Lesson 18

1 Decodable **Story**

Shadow in the Snow

by Nancy Furstinger
illustrations by Jesse Reisch

2 Genre: Realistic Fiction

Snow Surprise

by Lisa Campbell Ernst

3 Genre: Nonfiction Article

The Snowflake Man

Shadow in the Snow

by Nancy Furstinger

illustrated by Jesse Reisch

"Follow me, Shadow,"
yells Jess. "Let's play
in the snow!"

"Look at that black crow,"
Jess grins. "He soaks up sun
and sings all day."

A rabbit rests by an oak tree.
Shadow sniffs the snow. He
thinks he is on a hunt.

Jess tucks her chin under her yellow
coat. Snow blows off a branch and
onto her hat. "Shadow!" she calls.

A rowboat sits on a pond. "In spring, we'll row that boat on the water," Jess tells Shadow.

Jess zips along a hilltop on her sled.
Shadow runs with Jess.

"Let's have a snack, Shadow. I will eat an apple muffin, and you can drink a bowl of milk. Then let's go back and play in the snow!"

Phonics Skill

Words with <u>ow</u> and <u>oa</u>

R1.10
R1.12

The letters **ow** can stand for the long **o** sound, as in the words **bowl** and **snow**.

bowl   **snow**

The letters **oa** can also stand for the long **o** sound, as in the words **goat** and **road**.

goat   **road**

 CALIFORNIA STANDARDS
ENGLISH-LANGUAGE ARTS STANDARDS—Reading 1.10 Generate the sounds from all the letters and letter patterns, including consonant blends and long- and short-vowel patterns (i.e., phonograms), and blend those sounds into recognizable words; **Reading 1.12** Use knowledge of vowel digraphs and r-controlled letter-sound associations to read words.

Look at each picture. Read the words.
Tell which word names the picture.

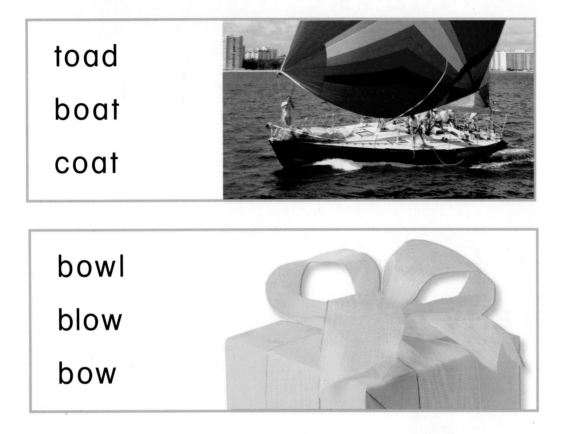

toad

boat

coat

bowl

blow

bow

 www.harcourtschool.com/reading

Try This!

Read the sentences.

I put on my coat to go out.
I could see the wind blow the
trees. I could see snow on the
road. I was glad I had my coat.

Words to Know

High-Frequency Words

R1.11

our

pretty

surprise

over

three

mouse

 CALIFORNIA STANDARDS
ENGLISH-LANGUAGE ARTS STANDARDS—Reading 1.11 Read common, irregular sight words (e.g., *the, have, said, come, give, of*).

There is lots of snow, and **our** yard looks **pretty**. I run out into the snow. I want to make a **surprise**.

Our dog runs so fast that he jumps **over** the steps! He runs with me into the snow. Then, he barks **three** times. Is Sport barking at a **mouse** or at some other animal?

 www.harcourtschool.com/reading

Snow Surprise
by Lisa Campbell Ernst

Realistic Fiction

R3.1

Genre Study

Realistic fiction stories are made-up, but the events could happen in real life.

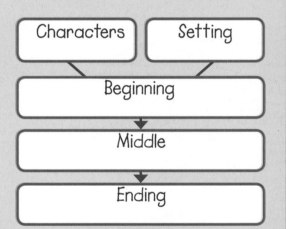

Characters	Setting
Beginning	
Middle	
Ending	

R2.6

Comprehension Strategy

Monitor Comprehension: Make Inferences Use clues from what you are reading and what you already know to help you understand the story.

CALIFORNIA STANDARDS
ENGLISH-LANGUAGE ARTS STANDARDS—
Reading 2.6 Relate prior knowledge to textual information;
Reading 3.1 Identify and describe the elements of plot, setting, and character(s) in a story, as well as the story's beginning, middle, and ending.

218

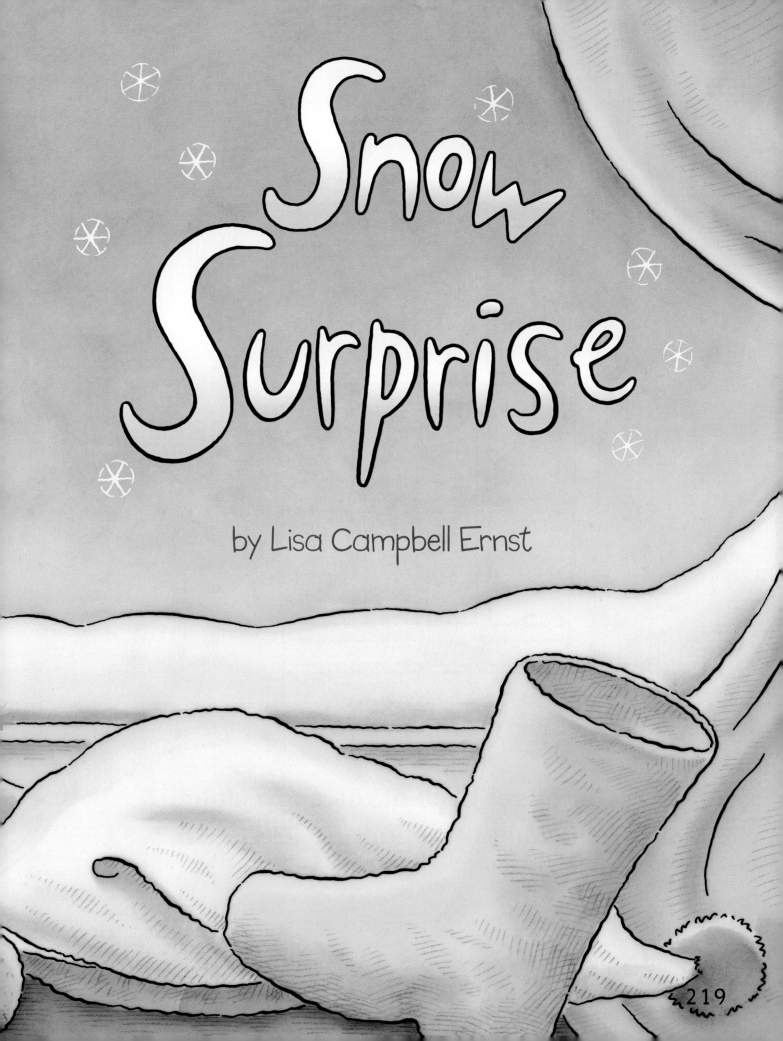

Snow Surprise

by Lisa Campbell Ernst

"Surprise! Look at the snow, Joan!"
yelled her little brother, Ben.

Joan looked out. The snow
was so pretty! Sport barked.

"I saw the snow first!
I saw the snow first!"
Ben sang.

Joan ran for her coat. "I'll show
you a snow surprise," she called to
Ben. Joan loaded her pockets with
all sorts of things.

"Don't look!" she said.
Then she ran out with Sport.

It was cold! Frost was on the
porch. Joan jumped off and
landed in the snow.

Sport ran and jumped in the snow, too. He nipped at the snow floating in the air.

"Come with me, Sport!" Joan called.

Joan packed snow into a small ball. Then she started rolling the ball.

"It's growing!" Joan yelled.

Joan made three snowballs. They were all in a row—big, bigger, and biggest.

Joan stacked the snowballs to make her snow surprise. She put one on top of the other.

She patted on more snow to fill
in the gaps. Sport barked at the
crows and other birds.

At last, Joan added the things
from her pockets. She had apples,
nuts, yellow corn, crusts of toast,
and more.

Sport got sticks. Joan used them to make arms. She put food for the birds in bowls. Then she loaned her own hat and scarf to the snow surprise.

"Our snow surprise is perfect,"
Joan said to Sport. She ran in
to get Ben.

Out in the yard, the birds saw corn and toast. The animals smelled nuts and apples.

What did Sport smell? He smelled trouble!

In a flash, there <u>was</u> trouble.
The birds snatched the food. The
animals munched. It was a mad
dash for the snacks!

Sport jumped at them all. The
snow surprise tipped. Then it fell
over with a THUD!

Joan led Ben out to show him
the surprise. She gasped. It was
not there!

"Oh, no," Joan groaned.

Ben clapped his hands. "A mouse!" he sang. "It's a snow mouse!"

Joan looked again. It <u>was</u> a mouse.

"Surprise!" she said.

Think Critically

R2.2
R2.6
R3.1
R3.2
W2.1

1 Why do you think the author wrote this story? AUTHOR'S PURPOSE/POINT OF VIEW

2 What are the steps for making Joan's snow surprise? DETAILS

3 Do you think the animals are happy that Joan is making a snow surprise? Why or why not? DRAW CONCLUSIONS

4 Think about the ending. What do you think Joan and Ben will do next?

MAKE INFERENCES

5 **WRITE** Write about something you made to surprise someone, or about a time someone surprised you.

WRITING RESPONSE

CALIFORNIA STANDARDS
ENGLISH-LANGUAGE ARTS STANDARDS—Reading 2.2 Respond to who, what, when, where, and how questions;
Reading 2.6 Relate prior knowledge to textual information; **Reading 3.1** Identify and describe the elements of plot,
setting, and character(s) in a story, as well as the story's beginning, middle, and ending; **Reading 3.2** Describe the roles
of authors and illustrators and their contributions to print materials; **Writing 2.1** Write brief narratives (e.g., fictional,
autobiographical) describing an experience.

Lisa Campbell Ernst

Lisa Campbell Ernst grew up in a family that loved books and sharing stories. So, she would draw pictures and make up stories about the animals in her neighborhood.

"I still love drawing animals! To know how to draw Sport, I watched my pets Fred and Elmo playing outside. I watched the wildlife in my backyard for the other animals, and my daughter Allison to draw Joan."

Snowflakes in Photographs
W. A. Bentley

Nonfiction

The Snowflake Man

Wilson Bentley *loved* snow! He loved looking at snowflakes, but they would melt. Then he found a way to keep his snowflakes. He took pictures of them!

Read what Wilson Bentley said about snow.

"I was born in 1865, and I can't remember a time I didn't love the snow."

▼ Wilson Bentley is using an old camera to take his famous pictures. He is known as "Snowflake Bentley."

"A snowstorm is always so exciting to me. I never know when I am going to find some wonderful prize."

"You asked how I catch my crystals. I do it with this little wooden tray. It is painted black so that the flakes will show against it."

"Usually they have six sides or six branches. And the six sides will be exactly the same."

"Each snowflake is as different from its fellows as we are from each other."

Connections

Comparing Texts

R2.2
R3.3
LS2.3

1 What was the most interesting thing you learned about snow from "Snow Surprise" or "The Snowflake Man"?

2 What other things do people do in the snow for fun?

3 Tell about something you made that did not turn out the way you expected.

Writing

Pretend that Joan made the snow surprise for you. Write a note to thank her for it.

> January 17, 20--
> Dear Joan,
>   Thank you for making the snow surprise for me. It looks like a giant mouse! How did you make it?
>   Your Pal,
>   Emma

CALIFORNIA STANDARDS
ENGLISH-LANGUAGE ARTS STANDARDS—Reading 1.10 Generate the sounds from all the letters and letter patterns, including consonant blends and long- and short-vowel patterns (i.e., phonograms), and blend those sounds into recognizable words; *(continued)*

Phonics

R1.10 R1.12

Make and read new words.

Start with **slow**.

Change **s** **l** to **r**.

Change **w** to **a** **d**.

Change **r** to **t**.

Change **d** to **s** **t**.

Fluency Practice

R1.16

Take turns reading pages of "Snow Surprise." Make the characters sound as if they are really talking to you.

"Come with me, Sport!"

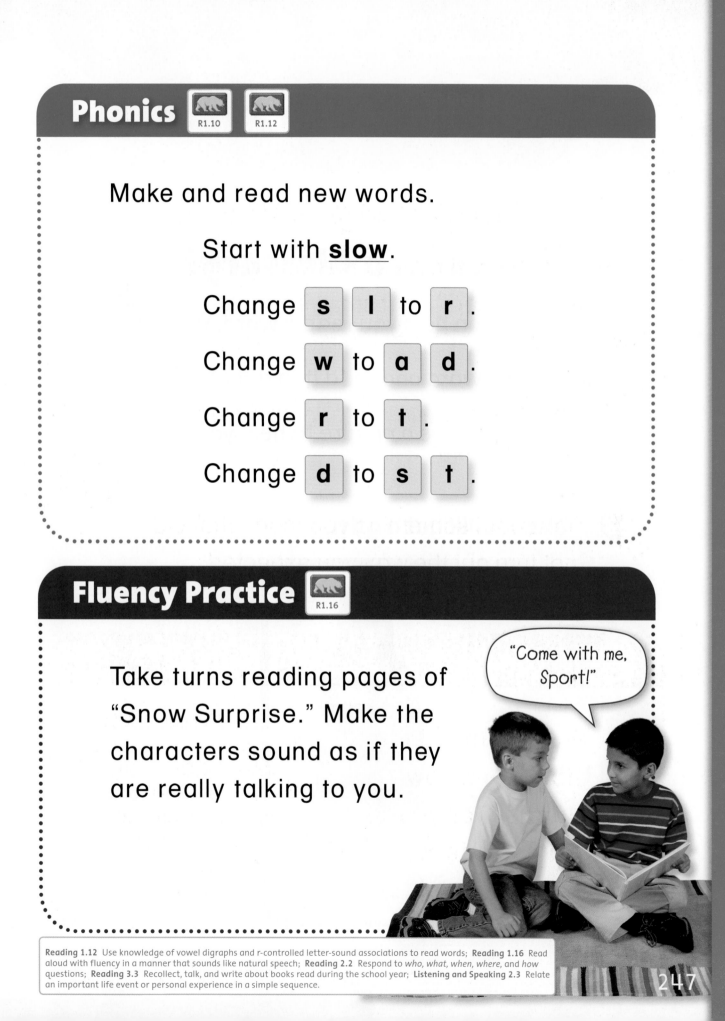

Reading 1.12 Use knowledge of vowel digraphs and r-controlled letter-sound associations to read words; **Reading 1.16** Read aloud with fluency in a manner that sounds like natural speech; **Reading 2.2** Respond to *who, what, when, where,* and *how* questions; **Reading 3.3** Recollect, talk, and write about books read during the school year; **Listening and Speaking 2.3** Relate an important life event or personal experience in a simple sequence.

Glossary

What Is a Glossary?

A glossary can help you read a word. You can

look up the word and read it in a sentence.

Some words have a picture to help you.

gift   Jill got a **gift.**

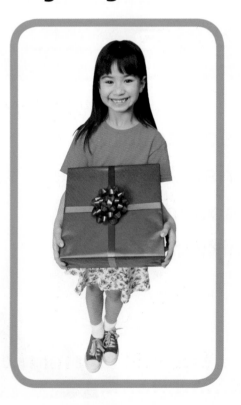

248

air   She can blow **air** to make bubbles.

books   Here is a stack of **books.**

buy   She will **buy** markers for school.

C

carry   He can **carry** the water.

F

family   There are two children in my **family.**

fly   He can make it **fly.**

friends   Emma and Beth are good **friends.**

house   I see a tree by the **house.**

know   We **know** how to add.

loud   This animal has a **loud** roar.

money   She has **money** on her desk.

mouse   A **mouse** is a very small animal.

N

name   His dog's **name** is Spot.

nice   She is **nice** to help.

O

over   **The ball went over his head.**

P

paint   **We have paint and brushes.**

paper   **This paper is pink.**

people   Many **people** went to the park.

play   Sal likes to **play** at the park.

pretty   The flowers are **pretty**.

R

rain   The **rain** fell hard.

read   I **read** a book with Granddad.

room   Jim has a clock in his **room.**

surprise   The gift was a **surprise.**

T

three   Here are **three** flowers.

W

watch   They **watch** for the bus to come.

work   The birds **work** on their nest.

writing   She is **writing** a list.

Decodable Stories Word Lists

The following words appear in the Decodable Stories in Book 1-3.

Lesson 13   "Rich Gets Big"

Word Count: 97

High-Frequency Words	Decodable Words*	
be	a	mitt
grow	an	Mom
he	and	more
now	big	not
see	**branch**	on
she	brings	**Patch**
the	calls	**pitch**
to	cannot	**porch**
wants	cat	**Rich**
was	**catch**	shelf
you	**chest**	sits
	for	small
	get	snapshots
	gets	stands
	has	tells
	his	that
	I	thinks
	inch	will
	is	wish
	it	with
	just	yes
	long	

*Words with /ch/*ch, tch* appear in **boldface** type.

Lesson 14   "Ann's Trip to the Stars"

Word Count: 120

High-Frequency Words	Decodable Words*	
cold	a	has
go	am	help
her	and	hot
my	Ann	I
play	Ann's	in
says	asks	is
the	back	it
to	**bark**	kit
you	**barks**	long
	Ben	**Mars**
	big	Mom
	blast	not
	block	off
	can	path
	Carl	red
	claps	rocks
	cloth	**sharp**
	crashes	ship
	Dad	stands
	dark	**stars**
	end	**start**
	far	**starts**
	fix	sun
	flash	thanks
	get	trip
	grin	will
	grins	with
	hall	yells
	hangs	yes

*Words with /är/*ar* appear in **boldface** type.

Lesson 15 "A Quiz for Brent"

Word Count: 116

High-Frequency Words	Decodable Words*	
find	a	is
happy	bed	it
he	big	it's
house	Brent	Mom
of	bucket	not
out	check	on
the	cloth	**quick**
to	Dad	**quilt**
too	desk	**quit**
what	did	**quiz**
	finish	red
	for	runs
	gets	small
	glad	soft
	got	tan
	Granddad	tells
	has	that
	him	think
	hint	will
	his	yard

*Words with /kw/*qu* appear in **boldface** type.

Lesson 16 "A Perfect Lunch"

Word Count: 145

High-Frequency Words	Decodable Words*	
come	a	Kit
comes	all	let's
day	and	Liz
do	ask	lunch
friends	Ben	Meg
have	**Bert**	Meg's
he	best	muffin
here	big	muffins
how	**bird**	next
looks	brim	**perfect**
my	bumps	**perhaps**
no	can	picks
now	charming	picnic
oh	corn	**serving**
out	**dirt**	sets
says	dishes	sips
she	drink	sit
the	drops	sits
they	fills	**skirt**
where	**first**	**squirt**
	for	**squirts**
	glass	tap
	grins	**third**
	hat	this
	her	trick
	his	twig
	hits	up
	in	will
	is	with
	it's	yells
	Jen	

*Words with /ûr/*er, ir* appear in **boldface** type.

Word Count: 107

High-Frequency Words	Decodable Words*	
animals	a	**jangle**
do	all	**jingle**
elephant	an	**juggle**
elephants	and	jump
family	balls	**jungle**
have	bells	kick
join	best	**little**
make	big	pick
soon	birds	pins
the	**bubbles**	**purple**
they	can	red
who	cannot	ring
you	catch	run
	cats	**sparkle**
	chirp	spin
	chuckle	start
	contest	stomp
	foxes	that
	fun	tricks
	giggle	**tumble**
	glitter	turn
	hats	**wiggle**
	in	will
	is	win

*Words with /əl/-*le* appear in **boldface** type.

Lesson 18 "Shadow in the Snow"

Word Count: 125

High-Frequency Words	Decodable Words*	
by	a	**oak**
day	all	off
eat	along	on
go	an	pond
have	and	rabbit
he	apple	rests
look	at	**row**
me	back	**rowboat**
of	black	runs
onto	**blows**	**Shadow**
play	**boat**	sings
she	**bowl**	sits
the	branch	sled
tree	calls	snack
water	can	sniffs
we'll	chin	**snow**
you	**coat**	**soaks**
	crow	spring
	drink	sun
	follow	tells
	grins	that
	hat	then
	her	thinks
	hilltop	tucks
	hunt	under
	I	up
	in	will
	is	with
	Jess	**yellow**
	let's	yells
	milk	zips
	muffin	

*Words with /ō/ow, oa appear in **boldface** type.

English-Language Arts Content Standards

READING

1.0 **Word Analysis, Fluency, and Systematic Vocabulary Development**
Students understand the basic features of reading. They select letter patterns and know how to translate them into spoken language by using phonics, syllabication, and word parts. They apply this knowledge to achieve fluent oral and silent reading.

Concepts About Print

1.1 Match oral words to printed words.

1.2 Identify the title and author of a reading selection.

1.3 Identify letters, words, and sentences.

Phonemic Awareness

1.4 Distinguish initial, medial, and final sounds in single-syllable words.

1.5 Distinguish long- and short-vowel sounds in orally stated single-syllable words (e.g., *bit/bite*).

1.6 Create and state a series of rhyming words, including consonant blends.

1.7 Add, delete, or change target sounds to change words (e.g., change *cow* to *how*; *pan* to *an*).

1.8 Blend two to four phonemes into recognizable words (e.g., */c/a/t/* = cat; */f/l/a/t/* = flat).

1.9 Segment single-syllable words into their components (e.g., cat = /c/a/t/; splat = /s/p/l/a/t/; rich = /r/i/ch/).

Decoding and Word Recognition

1.10 Generate the sounds from all the letters and letter patterns, including consonant blends and long- and short-vowel patterns (i.e., phonograms), and blend those sounds into recognizable words.

1.11 Read common, irregular sight words (e.g., *the, have, said, come, give, of*).

1.12 Use knowledge of vowel digraphs and r-controlled letter-sound associations to read words.

1.13 Read compound words and contractions.

1.14 Read inflectional forms (e.g., *-s, -ed, -ing*) and root words (e.g., *look, looked, looking*).

1.15 Read common word families (e.g., *-ite, -ate*).

1.16 Read aloud with fluency in a manner that sounds like natural speech.

Vocabulary and Concept Development

1.17 Classify grade-appropriate categories of words (e.g., concrete collections of animals, foods, toys).

2.0 **Reading Comprehension**
Students read and understand grade-level-appropriate material. They draw upon a variety of comprehension strategies as needed (e.g., generating

and responding to essential questions, making predictions, comparing information from several sources.) The selections in *Recommended Literature, Kindergarten Through Grade Twelve* illustrate the quality and complexity of the materials to be read by students. In addition to their regular school reading, by grade four, students read one-half million words annually, including a good representation of grade-level-appropriate narrative and expository text (e.g., classic and contemporary literature, magazines, newpapers, online information). In grade one, students begin to make progress toward this goal.

Structural Features of Informational Materials

2.1   Identify text that uses sequence or other logical order.

Comprehension and Analysis of Grade-Level-Appropriate Text

2.2   Respond to *who, what, when, where,* and *how* questions.

2.3   Follow one-step written instructions.

2.4   Use context to resolve ambiguities about word and sentence meanings.

2.5   Confirm predictions about what will happen next in a text by identifying key words (i.e., signpost words).

2.6   Relate prior knowledge to textual information.

2.7   Retell the central ideas of simple expository or narrative passages.

3.0 Literary Response and Analysis

Students read and respond to a wide variety of significant works of children's literature. They distinguish between the structural features of the text and the literary terms or elements (e.g., theme, plot, setting, charcters). The selections in *Recommended Literature, Kindergarten Through Grade Twelve* illustrate the quality and complexity of the materials to be read by students.

Narrative Analysis of Grade-Level-Appropriate Text

3.1 Identify and describe the elements of plot, setting, and character(s) in a story, as well as the story's beginning, middle, and ending.

3.2 Describe the roles of authors and illustrators and their contributions to print materials.

3.3 Recollect, talk, and write about books read during the school year.

WRITNG

1.0 Writing Strategies

Students write clear and coherent sentences and paragraphs that develop a central idea. Their writing shows they consider the audience and purpose. Students progress through the stages of the writing process (e.g., prewriting, drafting, revising, editing successive versions).

Organization and Focus

1.1 Select a focus when writing.

1.2 Use descriptive words when writing.

Penmanship

1.3 Print legibly and space letters, words, and sentences appropriately.

2.0 Writing Applications (Genres and Their Characteristics)

Students write compositions that describe and explain familiar objects, events, and experiences. Student writing demonstrates a command of standard American English and the drafting, research, and organizational strategies outlined in Writing Standard 1.0.

Using the writing strategies of grade one outlined in Writing Standard 1.0, students:

2.1 Write brief narratives (e.g., fictional, autobiographical) describing an experience.

2.2 Write brief expository descriptions of a real object, person, place, or event, using sensory details.

WRITTEN AND ORAL ENGLISH LANGUAGE CONVENTIONS

The standards for written and oral English language conventions have been placed between those for writing and for listening and speaking because these conventions are essential to both sets of skills.

1.0 Written and Oral English Language Conventions

Students write and speak with a command of standard English conventions appropriate to this grade level.

Sentence Structure

1.1 Write and speak in complete, coherent sentences.

Grammar

1.2 Identify and correctly use singular and plural nouns.

1.3 Identify and correctly use contractions (e.g., *isn't, aren't, can't, won't*) and singular possessive pronouns (e.g., *my/mine, his/her, hers, your/s*) in writing and speaking.

Punctuation

1.4 Distinguish between declarative, exclamatory, and interrogative sentences.

1.5 Use a period, exclamation point, or question mark at the end of sentences.

1.6 Use knowledge of the basic rules of punctuation and capitalization when writing.

Capitalization

1.7 Capitalize the first word of a sentence, names of people, and the pronoun *I*.

Spelling

1.8 Spell three- and four-letter short-vowel words and grade-level-appropriate sight words correctly.

1.0 Listening and Speaking Strategies

Students listen critically and respond appropriately to oral communication. They speak in a manner that guides the listener to understand important ideas by using proper phrasing, pitch, and modulation.

Comprehension

1.1 Listen attentively.

1.2 Ask questions for clarification and understanding.

1.3 Give, restate, and follow simple two-step directions.

Organization and Delivery of Oral Communication

1.4 Stay on the topic when speaking.

1.5 Use descriptive words when speaking about people, places, things, and events.

2.0 Speaking Applications (Genres and Their Characteristics)

Students deliver brief recitations and oral presentations about familiar experiences or interests that are organized around a coherent thesis statement. Student speaking demonstrates a command of standard American English and the organizational and delivery strategies outlined in Listening and Speaking Standard 1.0.

Using the speaking strategies of grade one outlined in Listening and Speaking Standard 1.0, students:

2.1 Recite poems, rhymes, songs, and stories.

2.2 Retell stories using basic story grammar and relating the sequence of story events by answering *who, what, when, where, why,* and *how* questions.

2.3 Relate an important life event or personal experience in a simple sequence.

2.4 Provide descriptions with careful attention to sensory detail.

Acknowledgments

For permission to reprint copyrighted material, grateful acknowledgment is made to the following sources:

Mari Evans: "I Can" from *Singing Black* by Mari Evans. Published by Reed Visuals, 1979.

Marian Reiner, on behalf of the Boulder Public Library Foundation: "Caterpillars" from *Cricket in a Thicket* by Aileen Fisher. Text copyright © 1963 by Aileen Fisher.

Photo Credits

Placement Key: (t) top; (b) bottom; (l) left; (r) right; (c) center; (bg) background; (fg) foreground; (i) inset

12 (c) Images.com/Corbis; 15 (b) Don Farrall / Getty Images; 24 Creatas Images/JupiterImages; 6 Petr RF/Shutterstock; 31 (inset) Peter J Bryant/ BPS/Stone/Getty Images; 41 (bg) Raul Touzon/National Geographic/ Getty Images; 42 (c) Photo 24/Brand X Pictures /JupiterImages; 53 (bl) Royalty Free/Corbis; 62 Ariel Skelley/Corbis; 62 Ingram Publishing /SuperStock; 62 Purestock /SuperStock; 63 Masterfile Royalty Free; 64 (t) image100/SuperStock; 93 (br) RubberBall Productions/PictureQuest; 140 David S April RF/Shutterstock; 102 Christopher Bissell/Stone/Getty Images; 103 Geoff Dann/Dorling Kindersley/Getty Images; 103 Markus Botzek/zefa/Corbis; 129 (br) Ariel Skelley/Blend Images/Picture Quest; 138 BananaStock/Alamy; 161 (c) © Gray Crabbe / Enlightened images; 161 (tc) © Tim Hursley / SuperStock; 161 (c) Ian Dagnall/Alamy; 161 (tc) Jeremy Woodhouse/Digital Vision/Getty Images; 165 (b) Art Wolfe/Getty Images; 176 Katya Arnold; 176 (t) tadija/Shutterstock; 200 (fg) Andy Rouse/NHPA; 201 (cr) Cris Haigh/Alamy; 201 (tr) Matthias Clamer/Getty Images; 201 (br) ZSSD/Minden Pictures; 202 (t) tadija RF/Shutterstock; 205 (l) Stockdisc/Getty Images; 214 (c) Allan Davey / Masterfile; 214 (c) Ray Ooms / Masterfile; 214 Eline Spek/Shutterstock; 215 Royalty-Free/Corbis; 215 SuperStock; 216 (t) Pepe Ramirez/ Shutterstock; 240- 242, 243-245 (t) Peter Wolf/ Wolf Multimedia Studio; 243 (br) Historic NWS Collection/National Oceanic and Atmospheric Administration/Department of Commerce; 246 (t) OlgaLis/Shutterstock. All other photos © Harcourt School Publishers. Harcourt photos provided by Harcourt Index, Harcourt IPR, and Harcourt Photographers: Weronica Ankarorn, Eric Camden, Doug DuKane, Ken Kinsie, April Riehm and Steve Williams.

Illustration Credits

Cover Art; Laura and Eric Ovresat, Artlab, Inc.